CREATURELY

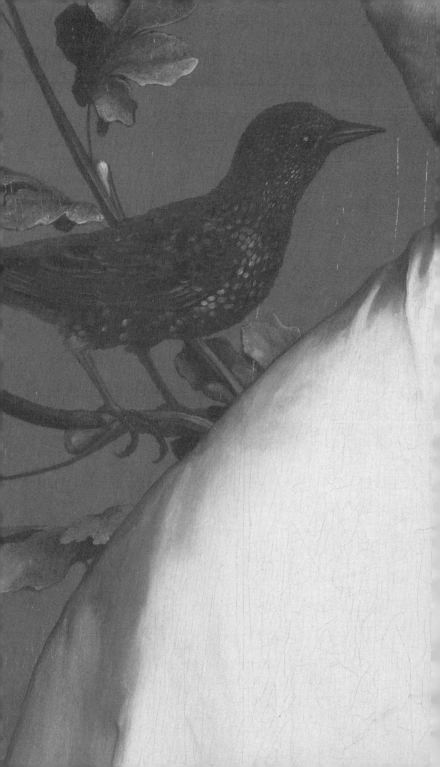

Creaturely

AND OTHER ESSAYS

DEVIN JOHNSTON

TURTLE POINT PRESS

NEW YORK 2009

The creatures will come creeping back —
not as gods transmogrified, but as themselves.

DAVID MALOUF, *An Imaginary Life*

This little book is largely made up of digressions, departures from a life spent too much indoors. In keeping with the etymology of the word *digression*, I drafted these essays walking around St. Louis and its environs, where I have lived since 2001. As Henry David Thoreau would say, I acted for a time as self-appointed inspector of thunderstorms and starlings, sycamores and squirrels, making my daily rounds. Weedy species and volunteers — common forms of life, opportunists like ourselves — I took as my particular charge. I sought out their local haunts, imagining what they saw, heard, smelled, tasted, and felt. En route, a poem would often come to mind, my private anthology serving as a wayward field guide to whatever I found. In that sense, the poems quoted here are less objects of study than "equipment for living" (in Kenneth Burke's phrase).

Wandering with my dog, I have passed whole afternoons—gray January days, humid August days in the white noise of air-conditioning compressors—without encountering another person. Though the resulting book teems with creaturely life, other people rarely enter it directly. However, as engagements with the world, these essays are inextricable from some of my friendships. They extend memorable conversations with Bob Adamson and Juno Gemes, Brian Calvin and Siobhan McDevitt, Jeff Clark, Lisa Jarnot, Michael O'Leary, Peter O'Leary, Tom Pickard, Pam Rehm, Eirik Steinhoff, and John Tipton. Above all, Andrea Dunn's curiosity —with binoculars at the ready—inspired these forays across the border between humans and animals.

ACKNOWLEDGMENTS

Some of these essays have previously appeared in *Denver Quarterly*, *Orion*, and *Threepenny Review*.

I am grateful to the following publishers and persons for use of copyrighted material: Faber and Faber Ltd. and Viking Penguin, a division of Penguin Group (USA) Inc., for "The Sycamore" from *The Poems of Marianne Moore*, edited by Grace Schulman. Copyright © 2003 by Marianne Craig Moore, Executor of the Estate of Marianne Moore. Flood Editions for "Dusk" from *Hole in the Wall: New and Selected Poems* by Tom Pickard. Copyright © 2002 by Tom Pickard. Paper Bark Press for "Crows in Afternoon Sunlight" from *Mulberry Leaves: New and Selected Poems, 1970–2001* by Robert Adamson. Copyright © 2001 by Robert Adamson. University of California Press for "A monster owl" from *Collected Works* by Lorine Niedecker, edited by Jenny Penberthy. Copyright © 2002 by the Regents of the University of

California. A. P. Watt Ltd. on behalf of Gráinne Yeats for "To a Squirrel at Kyle-na-no" by William Butler Yeats.

Finally, I wish to thank Andrew Katz for help in copy-editing this book.

Creaturely

*A dunghill at a distance sometimes smells
like musk, and a dead dog like elder-flowers.*

SAMUEL TAYLOR COLERIDGE, *Notebooks*

It's a bright morning in early May. I leash Chester, our border collie, and head south on Louisiana Avenue, the street empty of other pedestrians. We take a desultory pace, like an old couple out for a stroll. Leash looped around my forearm, I look up, watching for birds, while Chester sticks to the lawn strip with his head down, occasionally stopping to cock his leg. His eyes are focused on the grass a few feet ahead, but absently; all attention is clearly concentrated in his nasal cavity. A thick stand of clover, the lower branches of a holly tree, and a wax-paper sandwich wrapper offer absorbing subjects for inspection.

Not everything draws his nose. After last night's rain,

the white azalea bush is heavy as cake frosting, its perfume thick. But it does not pertain to him. Likewise, the sweet smell of hops from the Budweiser Brewery, a lawn mower's clippings, and gasoline sloshed on the curb are olfactory background to be filtered out. He sifts the world for relevant signs.

Predictably, traces of urine and old turds are Chester's expertise: he examines each stain as if under a glass slide. Although I may catch a whiff of ammonia and lilac in cat piss, or yeast and jasmine in dog feces, expressive variety is lost on me. But a dog's nasal membranes, the size of a handkerchief unfurled, allow for subtle gradations and recognitions of what has passed.

It's a quiet, local gossip. Surely this trace was left by Poncho, Mr. Hubbard's dog, got loose again and ambling up and down the block, in a quandary as to how to spend his freedom. Beyond where and when, the trace may carry somatic information of infection, unhappiness, or a full belly. Insides are out, nothing is private. When Chester inhales, or touches his tongue to a dried droplet on a violet leaf, the outside is in again.

Smell and taste differ radically from vision and hearing in conveyance. Whereas the latter are stimulated by energetic phenomena, smells are carried by plumes of particulate matter on air currents, dispersing as the air stirs. As matter blown apart, smells invade our sensorium and adhere. Apart from our shame or revulsion, smell is in this respect more intimate than sight or hearing, closer to touch. It stirs wants and fears beneath what the eye can see or intellect discern.

"Is it even possible to think of somebody in the past?" the writer Aidan Higgins asks. The source may be long gone; the dog that ambled by at noon sleeps on a chair. Yet its smell remains a palpable presence. We are so accustomed to the certainties of sight that olfaction baffles time. It ripples through the world like books or dreams.

From an open window, the smell of pine cleanser rides a wave of cooler air onto the sidewalk. Following an etymological trail, I find that the word *smell* relates to the Slavic *smola*, which means "resin" or "pitch." Pine has long been a demonifuge, driving away evil spirits with purifying smoke. Household cleaning products, household gods.

If sight is evidential (I saw it with my own eyes), smell moves us closer to essences. I have known some people who exude the scent of chlorine or vanilla with sweat, a faint but indelible association. In Greek thought, an inner fire distills essences from the more volatile portion of a being. As Herakleitos writes, "The stuff of the psyche is a smoke-like substance of finest particles that gives rise to all other things; its particles are of less mass than any other substance and it is constantly in motion." Somewhat more mysteriously, he adds, "In Hades psyches perceive each other by smell alone." For the Greeks, bodily odors and breath carry the effluvia of essence, undiminished while the organism lives, the sole continuity of the psyche when it dies. They burnt offerings, making taste and smell primary to their experience of divinity. Such was the case with most of the ancient world, from Han to Heliopolis. In Exodus, the Lord goes so far as to give Moses a detailed recipe for incense, promising to meet him in the smoke.

Perfume emerged as a variation on incense, *per fume* meaning "by smoke." Yet applied to the body, it assumed increasingly erotic associations. A rose, eros. "A bundle of myrrh is my beloved to me," the poet writes in the Song of Solomon; "Whenas the meanest part of her, / Smells like the maiden-Pomander," Robert Herrick claims of Lady Abdy. Perfumes both mask and amplify the pheromones, carrying hints of something vaguely urinous. The bass notes of many perfumes have drawn from the bowels of sperm whales and civets or the glands of Himalayan musk deer. Walking into any steak house, one could detect the steroidal odors of exotic creatures on both men and women; only the human is forbidden. Beneath the light and quick scent of hyacinth, sage, cinnamon, or sandalwood, a warm animal smell lingers.

———

Human olfaction is full of such preoccupations, deflections, and echoes. We have little language proper to smell, only makeshift analogies that take on currency through volatility. On my daily walks, pipe tobacco from a screened porch recalls pot roast, and I find that nitrogen is a prominent element in each. As I pass The Blackthorn, its beery floor brings to mind cheddar cheese, and diacetyl may be the shared compound. But such links hardly amount to a system of classification or taxonomy. Confronted by airplane glue I might say "unguent" or, synesthetically, "aluminum"; whether these are circumstantial or chemical associations I cannot say.

In the vast dark of olfaction, only cooking, wine, and perfume are illuminated by science as well as intuition. Yet even in these fields, characterizations remain empirical and exploratory. The scientist Luca Turin has described one perfume as "brilliant, at once edible (chocolate) and refreshingly toxic (caspirene, coumarin)." Perfumery is replete with such oxymorons intended to project social desire, a devil for every angel. For wines, most descriptors are suffixed nouns: buttery, grassy, oaky, earthy. Like the painter Giuseppe Arcimboldo, the wine connoisseur fabricates composite portraits from flowers, fruits, and vegetables. We do not find ourselves in an order of things but rather in a constellation of metaphors.

Each person accretes a private concordance of olfactory associations over the course of a lifetime. The resemblances are unstable, often sparked by emotional resonance and secondary associations. In this respect, smell is tightly woven into the fabric of consciousness.

At some depth, our notions of the world must be founded on odors—a familiar world of milk, sweat, skin, and detergents—from before the eyes could focus.

The poet Robert Duncan writes of butterflies "in warm currents of news floating,/flitting into areas of aroma,/tracing out of air unseen roots and branches of sense / I share in thought." Aromas have their own argot, a chemical code that triggers unconscious impulses in the nervous system. I get the news with each inhalation but have few words for it. We know more than we know but have no means to measure the extent of our partic-ipation in the world.

———

In literature, smell and taste often stand in for the mute fact of lived experience. Though I cannot verify the claim, I suspect that the chemical senses can be found most often in works of autobiography or memoir. Mar-cel Proust, after all, wrote thousands of pages on the flavor of a *petit madeleine* soaking in tea and what memories it evokes. The taste and its associations are in-extricable yet ultimately incommunicable. As Proust writes, "The past is hidden somewhere outside the realm, beyond the reach of intellect, in some material object (in the sensation which that material object will give us) of which we have no inkling." In *A Remembrance of Things Past*, as in a great many books, odors come to us from a lost world with sad voluptuousness. Each taste or smell bears no substitute, enters no general currency, but longs for a more perfect articulation. In melancholic reverie, we want no approximations of what we love.

I am reminded of a passage in Basil Bunting's poem "Briggflatts," subtitled "an autobiography," in which he enumerates the pleasures of the senses. Taste comes first in the list, followed by sound and touch:

> It tastes good, garlic and salt in it,
> with the half-sweet white wine of Orvieto
> on scanty grass under great trees
> where the ramparts cuddle Lucca.

The intimacy of taste sympathetically encourages an intimacy in the language, resulting in the apt but unexpected word "cuddle" applied to city fortifications. Yet at the end of this list, sight introduces a gap of self-consciousness that can never be mended:

It looks well on the page, but never
well enough. Something is lost
when wind, sun, sea upbraid
justly an unconvinced deserter.

Looking and writing are sure but distancing, Bunting suggests. We abandon full participation in sensual experience for its representation. According to the poem, "something" lost may be the smell of burning applewood or the twitter of a lark; meanwhile, the mason's chisel "spells a name / naming none, / a man abolished."

"Briggflatts" records a counterpoint or argument between the senses, each of which accords differently with time. Doubtless we carry time with us, each cell a tiny clock. Yet the experience of it comes to us in plumes, waves, particles, and through impulses of the nervous system. A bull chases hurdling shadows (sight), knots of applewood smolder all day (smell), pulse determines pace (touch), and a wagon rattles in polyrhythm:

harness mutter to shaft,
felloe to axle squeak,
rut thud the rim,
crushed grit.

In these various senses of duration, animals figure prominently, a bestiary of bull, lark, vulture, cormorant, slowworm, tortoise, starfish, hermit crab, salmon, bass, rat, bear, and border collie. To test the amplitude of time beyond human scale, creatures are enlisted as emissaries of the senses. At high altitude, ocean depths, or close to the earth, they enact modes of attention. If anthropomorphism interprets the world in human terms, we can with patience arrive at its inversion: not humanizing but creaturely.

———

It's a warm evening in early June. As we walk south on Louisiana Avenue, Chester catches the scent of something—who knows what—upwind: his nose tilts into the air, nostrils flaring, accurate lips slightly parted. Meanwhile, I watch the sky for birds. Above Roosevelt High, a pair of red-tailed hawks spiral on updrafts into the clouds. A starling trails behind them, hectoring the male with jabs at its slick fan of tail feathers. But having made its point, or simply half-hearted, the starling soon descends. As the world pours away, the hawks enter silence and damp air. Loose and indifferent, their wheeling dilates with ascent; aloof and aloft, they are all eyes. The sun's lost to me behind roofs of houses, the whole street filled with shadow. But a thousand feet up, the sun must ride the tree line of Tower Grove Park, daylight for a quarter-hour more. Though witness to each other, our days are not the same.

Crows in Winter

On the south side of St. Louis, between the concrete piers of Interstate 64-40 and the light-rail tracks, there runs an industrial corridor fallen into desuetude.

Winding slowly through, I pass a massive Missouri National Guard armory from the 1920s, abandoned with all its windows broken and bulbs burnt out. I once heard that Charles Lindbergh manufactured experimental planes in this building, before his famous flight. Next door, the Famous-Barr warehouse looks bleached in the late-afternoon sun, with its cinder blocks and windows uniformly whitewashed. Occasionally, white trucks back up to its loading docks. I turn onto Sarpy Avenue and pull to a stop across from the St. Louis Automatic Sprinkler Company and the (sinisterly named) Rentokil office, its facade so ambiguous it could be defunct. A nine of clubs lies on the curb.

Bare in winter, a raggedy stand of trees—alder, walnut, and sumac—backs up to the highway. Every branch holds a dozen crows, oddly fluttering like dead leaves. They number in the hundreds, with more arriving from the west as the sun falls. Yet the birds are surprisingly quiet: their wings softly creak as they settle down for the night, with occasional caws from younger males jockeying for a branch. In the midst of the colony, I can hear the dry snap of an icicle.

Within the city, so many birds react to human shadows with mild, directionless anxiety: sparrows agitating a bush, starlings darting between telephone wires. Yet these crows maintain a steely alertness at my presence. With neither a cat's sleepy perturbation nor a dog's frenzy, crows are close but unfamiliar. They know more of us than we of them.

———

Colonies assemble in late autumn, holding court and exchanging information through the winter months, dispersing each spring. During the day, they flicker past at the edge of attention, spreading news of a dead dog recently discovered or a Dumpster with fish heads. Their adaptive, nimble minds are not caged by patterns of behavior, and so their flight patterns are constantly in flux. Occasionally, an entire colony shifts, leaving no forwarding address. Finding Sarpy Avenue empty one evening, I follow the loping flight of one crow north of the interstate, to a fluttering tree on Sarah Street. What disturbance or attraction brought them here, I can't determine.

We know of the symbiotic relationship between crows and wolves, their caws alternating with howls across some northern pine barrens. But crows are now linked with cities and humans on a massive scale: they attend to what we shy away from, darkening the wastelands of our inattention. Crows in my neighborhood have learned the city's infrastructure with a detail unmatched by human residents: the routes and schedules of garbage trucks, the tides of traffic, and the timers of streetlights. In so many spaces we have made—concrete islands, the crow's nests of telephone poles, war zones—they are more at home than we could ever be. Crows effortlessly merge with smoke and cloud in the dense cross-hatching of an etching. As the foreboding book of Zephaniah prophesies, after the destruction of Nineveh, "the owl shall hoot in the window, / the raven croak on the threshold." I am reminded that *raven* can refer to the black precipitate of alchemy, the *nigredo* or *caput corvi* associated with the Earth and chaos.

Alert and at ease in vicinities of death, crows suggest a grandeur of destruction. Masahisa Fukase captures this aspect of corvids in his book of black-and-white photographs, *The Solitude of Ravens*. (Despite this English title, most of the subjects appear to be jungle crows rather than ravens.)

Fukase's photographs of corvids began in 1976, on a train ride from Tokyo home to Hokkaido after his divorce. For a decade he dwelled on this desolate subject: the silhouette of a corvid's head, the shadow of its wing, the grainy shapes of five on a bare branch; crow eyes reflecting a strobe flash at night, constellations of them in a feathery pine; crow footprints and a dead crow with its eyes shut in the snow; a single crow crossing the billow of a smokestack, a train hurtling through an industrial landscape at dusk; distillate of crow against a winter sky; a country road on Rebun Island at night; a landfill incinerator on Dream Island; the shadow of four crows on pavement, in formation, like the broad-winged American B-52 bombers; the curled feet of a crow in flight.

Some photographs consist of little more than smothered light and emulsion, snow and the cold Pacific. In night shots particularly, crows function more as a swarming ground than a focal point.

Their sociable desolation recalls a Border ballad, "The Twa Corbies," in which two crows cheerfully discuss their prospect for dinner, a dead knight:

> "In behint yon auld fail dyke,
> I wot there lies a new-slain knight;
> And naebody kens that he lies there,
> But his hawk, his hound, and lady fair.
>
> "His hound is to the hunting gane,
> His hawk to fetch the wild-fowl hame,
> His lady's ta'en another mate,
> Sa we may make our dinner sweet.
>
> "Ye'll sit on his white hause-bane,
> And I'll pike out his bonny blue een:
> Wi' ae lock o' his gowden hair,
> We'll theek our nest when it grows bare."

The ballad entails dramatic irony on several levels. First, the knight's companions in life have quickly dispersed in new pursuits, with the strong implication of murder by the "lady fair." Only scavengers remain, dividing his remains with intimacy and even admiration. Second, we only know the knight's fate through the imaginative artifice of talking birds. Otherwise, "nane sall ken where he is gane" but the birds themselves.

Metaphor lies in wait, the world's hidden scaffolding; yet the living bird adapts and evades fixed associations. Now ominous, now jolly, it alights in the vicinity of meaning and moves on. As documented in Laura C. Martin's *The Folklore of Birds*, counting rhymes enumerate what crows might augur:

> One for sorrow, two for mirth,
> Three for a wedding, four for a birth.
> Five for silver, six for gold,
> Seven for a secret not to be told.
> Eight for heaven, nine for hell,
> And ten for the devil's own sel'.

So mysterious have we found their comings and goings, close at hand yet as remote as stars, black marks in the book of our own fate.

As I wander past Sarah Street, four crows drift overhead and across an empty lot, intent and leisurely. One lets out a slow "caw caw, caw caw" while on the wing, possibly alerting others to my presence. A feral and almost desperate joy inflects its call, a mild aggravation and insistence. Researchers have concluded that crows use a system of simple counting in their communications, with the number of calls—as well as their intonation and duration—structuring their alarms, threats, boasts, invitations, and so forth. A shorter sequence of clicks and ratcheting squawks bursts from beyond the tree tops, a terse but conversational response.

But what do I know of their tones or intentions? As the Australian poet Robert Adamson writes in "Crows in Afternoon Sunlight,"

> How close can a human get to a crow,
> how much do we know about them?
> It's good to know we'll never read their brains,
> never know what it means to be a crow.
>
> All those crow poems are about poets—
> none of them get inside the crow's head,
> preen or rustle, let alone fly on crow wings.
>
> No one knows what it is to sing crow song.

The song is itself an emotional cipher, never cracked by our own needs and wants. Our certainties cannot escape anthropomorphism; our confidence derives from metaphors stripped of sensuous power and particularity. As Adamson suggests, we don't know enough and never will. Yet our very words "preen and rustle" when we draw close.

What they say is what we say. Though I have never heard a crow speak a word, they are capable of learning human language as well as the sounds of dogs, hawks, owls, and automobiles. Edgar Allan Poe famously captures the uncanny mixture of automatism and oracle in such mimicry: "Quoth the Raven, 'Nevermore.'" As if to check and challenge their imitative powers, we post scarecrows in crop fields and tether balloons with huge eyes around trash dumps. Perhaps the ingenuity of both crows and humans inevitably results in traps, tricks, false fronts, and the glint of an otherwise hidden mechanism.

Such are the roots of culture for both species. In *Culture and Anarchy*, Matthew Arnold defines culture as that which "places human perfection in an *internal* condition, in the growth and predominance of our humanity proper, as distinguished from our animality." Yet, as animal behaviorists now tell us, culture is not limited to humans. It might include anything learned, any information not genetically transmitted. House cats instinctively pounce, but they only learn the art of killing from their mothers. This technique constitutes culture, though far from Arnold's "sweetness and light." It must always begin with a mimicry preceding comprehension; from there, a little darkness grows.

———

It is summer now. I stroll at ease in the forest of Fontainebleau outside Paris. Among the old hardwoods and rocky outcroppings, I intermittently encounter pockets of cool air—respite from the heat—as if emanating from a grotto. Dappled light filters through an oak canopy. On a trail flanked by dense fern, a carrion crow crunches a blue beetle. Startled by a gunshot, it rises to a branch to wait and watch. Perhaps a Prussian soldier has been killed in retreat, his corpse richly rotting in a steep ravine. Or else the Sun King has killed a stag deep in the wood, leaving a feast of gralloch after field dressing. Did the crows memorize conventions of the hunt, its fanfare and succeeding calls, the horn sounding *hal-lali* as the quarry fell?

The crow shifts slightly on the branch, its supple neck just visible because darker than the shadows around it.

Murmurations

This spring afternoon, a steady drizzle falls from a low ceiling of cloud. It brings oils to the surface of street and sidewalk, glazing the ubiquitous brick. At the end of my block, a starling hunkers down on a telephone wire, its feathers damp with an iridescent sheen of purple, blue, and green. Rain drips from its yellow beak. I whistle a tune as I approach, and the bird listens, arching its neck and cocking its head slightly from side to side. Another wings toward us from down the alley, tail tilted downward, wings compact and slick. The rhythm of a starling's undulating flight is unmistakable: three rapid strokes followed by a glide.

The stationary starling bursts into song. It rattles like a shaken can of spray paint, then modulates through a wolf whistle, a screech, the woof of a neighborhood bulldog, and a cardinal's liquid phrase. But this composite song arrives through a burr of distortion, dust on the phonograph needle. Though the sources are recognizable, it couldn't fool anyone. I linger a few moments to listen before heading home. Somewhere down the block, the manual crank on a lawn mower won't quite catch in the rain.

The starling, like its cousin the mynah bird, improvises a pastiche of motifs drawn from life. Apparently, an adult starling may collect sixty or more motifs from which to pick and choose. These snippets are altered, rearranged, and spliced into an explosive sequence. As with the displacement of our days in dreams, the starling's song follows a syntax we humans have not yet learned. Yet we can discern from what the bird absorbs what absorbs its attention: predators, rivals, anomalies, and mysteries.

A starling's echoes are not only expressive but also exploratory. Meredith West and Andrew King, animal behaviorists, suggest that some birds "use acoustic probes to test the contingent properties of their environment." To discover what a sound means, the mimic essays it on the air, gauging the effect of each stolen phrase on its fellow creatures. Watchful behind its repertoire, with a sharp lookout for interest and opportunity, the starling throws out a few notes of cardinal song. Perhaps it's an experiment on the level of tossing a stone into a lake.

Whatever its purposes, mimicry sealed the starling to us. Since Roman times, at least, starlings have been kept as pets. I wonder how anyone could room with such a raucous creature? Between bursts of song, their young often keep up endless, squishy calls like wet sneakers. Even mimicry must wear on the nerves in close quarters, despite its charm. Starlings have an impressive ability to master human utterances, repeating words and phrases, sometimes suggesting a connected discourse just out of hearing. In the first part of *Henry IV*, Hotspur invokes this facility, almost as a curse:

> He said he would not ransom Mortimer,
> Forbade my tongue to speak of Mortimer,
> But I will find him when he lies asleep,
> And in his ear I'll holla "Mortimer!"
> Nay, I'll have a starling shall be taught to speak
> Nothing but "Mortimer," and give it to him,
> To keep his anger still in motion.

The starling's repetitions would extend Hotspur's own insistence, his hammering obsession with honor, his harping on "Mortimer" until the name loses meaning. Hearing our words come back to us—defamiliarized, automatic—brings a glint of fear as well as fascination.

According to what has become a familiar story, Hotspur brought the starling to America. A drug manufacturer named Eugene Schieffelin decided that New York should be home to all the songbirds mentioned in Shakespeare and joined the American Acclimatization Society for that purpose. Such an enterprise—with nature as the stage for a pastoral charade—was in keeping with the imperial aspirations of the era. Just as pilgrims had brought dandelions for their salads, the Chinese ring-necked pheasant was introduced to Oregon as a game bird. With only a touch more frivolity, Schieffelin imported Shakespeare's thrushes and skylarks from England, though neither survived in our ecosystems. The starling proved a much greater success: around fifty pairs were released in Central Park in 1890 and 1891; within a century they reached the West Coast, with a population of two hundred million. This weedy species—adaptive generalists—can be found everywhere. Yet despite their harsh cries and whistles, starlings now fade into the background, rarely a subject in and of themselves.

Schieffelin must have been a literalist of literature, a fanatical reenactor, who would look up from a word to its referent. In that sense, his birds were an extremity of period staging. Their song is a performance of Mozart on rickety fortepiano.

———

In from the rain, I dry off the dog's sopping coat, hang up my own, and switch on Mozart's Piano Concerto in C Major, K. 467, a midcentury recording featuring Dinu Lipatti as the soloist. The quality of recording is warm, crackly, and muted. I am not transported to the Kunsthaus in Lucerne—where the live recording was made, as my liner notes indicate—but hovering on the surface of the sound. To cut the damp chill, I pour myself a finger of Jameson's whisky, its amber that of rainwater standing in a log. James Thomson has a paean to the stuff in his poem "Sunday Up the River":

> I have watered this, though a toothful neat
>   Just melts like cream down the throttle:
> But it's grand in the punch, hot, strong, and sweet:
>   Not a headache in a bottle.

A few lines later:

> Just a little, wee, wee, tiny sip!
> Just the wet of the bill of a starling!

Thomson may have settled on the starling, of all birds, to rhyme with "darling." But the image—its yellow bill dipped in a jigger—is vivid and plausible. Meanwhile, Mozart's music, like the rain, suggests a regularity just out of hearing.

According to Mozart's biographers, he had a pet starling of which he was inordinately fond. He purchased the bird in 1784 and buried it with a funeral procession and elegy three years later. The pomp of the occasion was partly farcical, following in a charming tradition of mourning pets that extends back to Roman times. Ovid wrote an elegy for Corrina's parrot, and Catullus more famously addressed one to "passer, deliciae meae puellae" (sparrow, my girl's delight). Despite the poem's rhetorical trappings, it is as much erotic as elegiac (Catullus enviously describes the sparrow in his lover's lap or at her breast). But Mozart's affection for the bird was real, apparently sealed when it learned a melodic theme from his Piano Concerto in G Major, K. 453. Vogel Star, as he called the bird, would whistle variations on the tune, altering a G-natural note to G-sharp and adjusting the rhythm very slightly. "Das war schön," that was beautiful, Mozart recorded in his notebook.

Some scholars have detected the influence of Vogel Star on Mozart's *Ein musikalischer Spass*, A Musical Joke, к. 522, completed shortly after the starling's death. In the piece, Mozart parodies the inept and pretentious tendencies of his contemporaries. But in its most striking features, *Ein musikalischer Spass* bears a curious resemblance to starling song: the illogical patchwork of stock material, discords in the French horns, asymmetry, and haphazard polytonality. Though exaggerated for comic effect, such aspects are in keeping with the studied irregularities and asymmetries that always drive Mozart's work. In that sense, *Ein musikalischer Spass* is deeply affectionate as well as mocking. Mozart had a starling's heart—absurd, bawdy, fierce, and tender. Mozart of the dirty joke, quick riposte, double entendre, and whistled melody.

———

Across the Mississippi, I turn off the interstate onto Illinois Route 3, heading north past desolate industrial towns, the river on my left and the Norfolk Southern line on my right. It's a stretch of road arrived at by following one bad idea after another, by men who have acquired a taste for strippers and roasted venison. Here, commerce mostly consists of the adult variety—the Discreet Hotel, Thunder Road, Roxy's Nightclub—or else a cinderblock daycare named Bo Peep. In a gravel lot, beside a burnt-out truck wash, a forlorn prostitute poses in cutoffs and a tank top. Incongruously, waste fields and boggy wetlands separate these businesses. Deer leap through scrubby windbreaks; on the shoulder of the road wild turkeys graze. Rusted chain-link and barbedwire fences enclose rail yards and abandoned factories.

I pause before the padlocked gates of Chemetco copper smelter. Until it was shut down early this century, it poured forth sludge, baghouse dust, refractory brick, and acids. Above its rusted roofs, where the smoke of industry once billowed, a shoal of starlings banks in the air. The dense, particulate flock almost merges with rain clouds in the late-afternoon light. They rush through dereliction, desperate joy set against a landscape of sadness. Their sheer exuberance forms a complex pattern, thousands together, like the rose of metal filings around a magnet. Elsewhere murmurations reach a million birds, storms of birds, concentric "ring angels" vast enough to register on radar screens. How they maneuver without colliding into one another remains a deep and abiding mystery.

If the single starling is a wonder of melodic invention, a flock of them constitutes harmonic counterpoint. Melody against melody, their simultaneous lines of flight cross without crashing. Perhaps they follow Baroque laws of relative motion, as the relation of bird to bird appears contrary, oblique, or similar, but rarely parallel. They intermittently form dense cluster chords as they crowd together. Beyond music, the murmuration functions as a particle mind, each bird a thought. Watching the flock, I begin to connect the dots.

But the resulting order appears less geometric than combustive. In a series of black-and-white photographs entitled "Murmur" (2005–6), Richard Barnes captures the flock as thermodynamic system. His high-contrast, ink-jet prints register the subject's protean shifts: a net against dense clouds, smothering light; a sooty finger descending from overcast skies, the dark massing of intention at its tip; the swirl of ink in water, a distant question mark; the semitransparent mantle of an organism, a smudged glass squid; a storm of projectiles across a suburb of Rome. In an article in the *New York Times*, Jonathan Rosen points out that the suburb forming the backdrop to many of these photographs was built by Mussolini for the *Esposizione Universale Romana*, a celebration of fascist Italy. Rosen augurs in these vast murmurations "something malign, a sort of avian Nuremberg rally" as individual will accedes to mass and force.

Others find in the flock a seamless merging of individual and collective energies. Such was the case during the anti-CPE uprisings in France during the spring of 2006. The controversial *contrat première embauche* permitted employers to fire French workers under the age of twenty-six without offering a reason for doing so. In the protests that followed, university students joined with trade unions in strikes and marches. The graffiti scrawled on brick walls and bridges read, "Avenir, je t'aimais bien" (future, I used to love you) and "Guerre à la tristesse" (war on sadness). Manifestoes cited starling flight as a model for political action. The radical group *Temps critiques* proclaimed, "The urban 'starling flight' movements, splitting up and heading in different directions to evade the police and then regrouping to strike or disrupt, combine collective effectiveness with individual creativity." For them, murmurations offered a model of "self-organization."

Meanwhile, I watch the starling flock pass southwest, out of sight over a stand of sycamores. The smelter's flues issue nothing more. Its slag yards lie preternaturally still, lost in the quiet concentration of acidic decay. Across the empty parking lot, a red-winged blackbird sounds its thin, high trill. Feeling the damp chill, with thoughts of dinner, I return to the car.

———

Further on, close to the river, another murmuration descends on its evening roost, a bare oak. Each bird glides smoothly downward with wings outstretched, intent on an empty few inches on which to perch. I think of "Dusk," a poem that Tom Pickard wrote in Newcastle, England, some forty years ago:

> at dusk in Grainger street
> the starlings leaf the trees
>
> they alight to the backfire
> of a motorbike

The poem coheres around its assonance of long vowels: *street*, *leaf*, and *trees* in the first couplet; *alight*, *backfire*, and *motorbike* in the second. Nearly rhymes, these sounds suggest a simultaneity of things that are not the same, a pattern—in the poem's form as well as in the dusk—just beyond our grasp.

As the cloud of birds descends, it becomes a concentrated darkness in the oak limbs. The starlings begin a dusk chorus, condensing all they have heard of relevance or curiosity. Just as dreamwork transforms the body's stimuli and residues of desire, the birds' song sifts the ambience of this day. Their chorus accrues much that we will never hear, learnt from unpopulated grain fields, parking lots, and unlivable spaces that we have built. It rises to a great cacophony against the last light before diminishing.

Second Sight

How do you know but ev'ry Bird that cuts the airy way,
Is an immense world of delight, clos'd by your senses five?

WILLIAM BLAKE, *The Marriage of Heaven and Hell*

A dozen starlings lie scattered on the lawn, their wings fanned out to absorb the heat of the sun, letting its ultraviolet rays burn away the microbes in their feathers. Occasionally one rises in agitation and stalks among the sunbathers, pecking at tail feathers, eye darting from one to another. Beneath the dark surface of the feathers—slick as a sheath of negatives—an explosion of stars extends outward from each of their beaks. These markings become larger and more widely spaced down the breast, expanding from small dashes to arrowheads. The pattern suggests the reverse of needlepoint, each bright mark a stitch. Or so it looks to me. What the starling sees is another matter.

Following Plato, Plotinus reflects, "Never did eye see the sun unless it had first become sunlike." Yet the breadth of the sun's spectrum that is visible to the human eye proves comparatively narrow. Our vision filters out much of the electromagnetic radiation bathing the Earth. We are entirely blind to the ultraviolet range of the spectrum, but most birds perceive these short wavelengths. As opposed to our trichromatic vision (red, green, and blue), birds have a fourth dimension to sight. Their colors are not simply refinements of our own but include hues entirely unknown to us, such as the secondary hues that result from mixing spectral lights of red or green with ultraviolet.

To approximate what the starling sees, we would have to hold a black light up to the world. Flowers would reveal new hieroglyphs, drawing bees to their pollen. Many black fruits would shine brilliantly, reflecting rays of near ultraviolet. Urine stains—the territorial markings of dogs and cats—would glow against grass or tree bark. Our usual perceptual values would be upended. To a bird's eye, the painted bunting may be no more vivid than a starling.

Evidence of the ultraviolet spectrum is present everywhere, alongside our lives yet hidden from us. In this sense, it resembles the fairyland found in legends of Ireland and Scotland. Robert Kirk, a seventeenth-century Highland minister, offers an intriguing account of fairy life in _The Secret Commonwealth_. These secret creatures have bodies "somewhat of the nature of a condensed cloud and best seen in twilight" by those with hypersensory vision. "Some have bodies or vehicles so spongeous, thin, and defaecat that they are fed by only sucking into some fine spirituous liquor that pierces like pure air and oil." Others, like birds, steal grains of corn from crofts. Again like birds, they speak only by way of high, clear whistles.

According to Kirk, the senses of these refined spirits are attuned to vibratory hints of distant events, even those yet to occur. In this respect, they share with animals the intuitive powers that we have lost:

> As birds and beasts, whose bodies are much used to the change of the free and open air, foresee storms, so those invisible people are more sagacious to under-

stand by the Book of Nature things to come than we who are pestered with the grosser dregs of all elementary mixtures and have our purer spirits choked by them.

Like the fairies themselves, "men of second sight" and seers of fairies have a spectral sensitivity that surpasses "the ordinary vision of other men." They witness the hidden world through improvements "resembling in their own kind the usual artificial helps of optic glasses (as prospectives, telescopes, and microscopes)." Robert Hooke, the father of microscopy and a close contemporary of Kirk, argues in *Micrographia* that such instruments might compensate for the human loss of both sensory perfection and Adamic knowledge. A century later, William Blake conceived of our fall from full sensory awareness in similar terms. In *The Marriage of Heaven and Hell*, he tells us that the senses were "enlarged and numerous" until contracted into five: "For man has closed himself up, till he sees all things thro' narrow chinks of his cavern." Kirk suggests that seers return us to those aspects of creation — angelic hierarchies, fairy worlds, spirit lives — otherwise lost on mundane sight.

Naturally enough, readers came to think of "the seer, my informer" as Kirk himself, so detailed were his insights into the habits and natures of fairies. He was, after all, his father's seventh son. According to legend, in 1692, Kirk finally disappeared into the tales he told. As Walter Scott relates in his *Letters on Demonology and Witchcraft*, Kirk was walking one evening in his nightgown on a Dun-shi, or fairy mount, when "he sank down in what seemed to be a fit of apoplexy, which the unenlightened took for death, while the more understanding knew it to be a swoon produced by the supernatural influence of the people whose precincts he had violated." His grave in Aberfoyle stands empty, we are told, and Kirk himself still "drees his weird in Fairyland." The ironic victim of his own imaginative forays, he persists in some alternate space and time.

———

After this interlude in the Secret Commonwealth, I step back into the yard. The sun sits directly overhead, intensely bright, darkening the green shadows of our walnut tree. A ruby-throated hummingbird rises from the roses and comes to rest on a telephone line. Perched there with wings folded, this tiny bird feels inapt, like a mixed metaphor. On the grass below, a starling stalks through the small flock to which it belongs. Its eye picks up intensive areas of iridescence on the throat and coverts of the other birds. They ruffle their feathers, flashing signals of sexual attraction or merely presence: "Here I am!" These patches cast off a brilliant sheen beside which much of the world must look dim.

Distantly to the west, high cumulonimbus clouds issue an ultimatum of thunder. Creatures of the yard stir with the cooler air currents. The starlings collect themselves—shaking out their feathers—and flit down the alley out of sight.

As science discovers the spectral sensitivities of birds, their sensory world proves alien to ours, their consciousness recessed from us. Though Hooke believed otherwise, our scientific instruments observe rather than close the distance between a starling's eye and my own. To gain a glimpse of the fairy world, one need only step on a seer's foot and look over his right shoulder. Perhaps in the process of time—as Kirk would say—we will find a rhyme, rune, or ritual to reveal the vibrant hues of ultraviolet light.

Specific Worlds

A squirrel leaping from bough to bough,
and making the wood but one wide tree for
his pleasure, fills the eye not less than a lion

RALPH WALDO EMERSON, "Art"

As I sit at the window this autumn afternoon, a pair of gray squirrels flows like smoke or water up a black walnut tree. They spiral up the trunk, scurry along a massive limb, and then jump to the nodding branch of a neighboring oak. For them, all motor processes appear at a reduced speed: the flashing interval from branch to branch seems leisurely. Theirs is a world of curved contours, or else points in air connected by fluid leaps. On a familiar path, they follow the ramifications of thought, floating on a viscous medium through the day's refractory mass. As John Burroughs observes in *Squirrels and Other Fur-Bearers*, their passage through the trees is "almost a flight."

Squirrels have a depth perception of ten feet or more. Beyond that farthest plane, flashing automobiles, a striding human, and the sun pass without any difference in depth. When I approach a squirrel on the lawn, it freezes until certain that I am getting closer as well as larger. Then it abruptly scurries off.

At the edge of domestic life, yet undomesticated, the lives of squirrels glance off our own. There is traffic between us. William Butler Yeats captures this closeness in "To a Squirrel at Kyle-na-no":

> Come play with me;
> Why should you run
> Through the shaking tree
> As though I'd a gun
> To strike you dead?
> When all I would do
> Is to scratch your head
> And let you go.

The squirrel reacts with comic paranoia, as if every human action holds sinister implications. But gentle Yeats would hardly justify such fears. In his *Reveries over Childhood and Youth*, he recalls the origin of his dismay at killing animals: "I fished for pike at Castle Dargan and shot at birds with a muzzle-loading pistol until somebody shot a rabbit and I heard it squeal. From that on I would kill nothing but the dumb fish." After the full rhyme of "head" with "dead," the final off-rhyme of "go" with "do" carries the force of this conviction. It is a manifestation of letting go.

Kyle-na-no, the wood of nuts, forms one of the seven woods in Coole Park, Lady Gregory's estate in the west of Ireland. In the opening lines of *The Shadowy Waters*, dedicated to Gregory, Yeats celebrates "sunnier Kyle-na-no, / Where many hundred squirrels are as happy / As though they had been hidden by green boughs / Where old age cannot find them." As the retreat of his great ally and companion, the seven woods appear in his poetry as spaces of friendship. Likewise, squirrels enter as figures of sheer exuberance and self-fulfilled energy, defying the strictures of society, dignity, and old age. Capering out of reach, they fulfill the tree-climbing aspirations of children. In "An Appointment," Yeats sets his own frustrated political ambitions against the squirrel's "fierce tooth and cleanly limb." As the poem ends, "No government appointed him." We can add squirrel to a bestiary in Yeats's work that would include horse, cat, hare, hawk, swan, and salmon. Yet for Yeats, the squirrel's significance can't be extricated from the green boughs that transport and hide it.

For the squirrels in our yard, the walnut tree forms the central, vertical axis of their world. In spring, they hang from their hind feet to gather green catkins. In autumn, they scamper through the branches with green walnuts. I observe one hunched on a broad branch, gnawing through the spongy husk and dropping its frittered remains to the lawn below. As it works, the squirrel holds its tail curled above its head for shade or privacy. The very word *squirrel* comes from the Greek *skia oura*, "shadow tail." As a covering as well as a means of balance, its tail harmonizes with the tree itself.

At the end of the day, a squirrel lies flat on a horizontal branch, the last sunlight revealing auburn tips to the fur on its back. It looks strangely like a dog at rest with its soft belly stretched against the bark. Nothing could be more at home.

At the St. Louis Zoo the other day, I watched a squirrel dodge between the slightly splayed legs of a giraffe. The squirrel's undulation was that of a shallow, traveling wave, transferring energy from tree to wall. By contrast, without its loping gait, the giraffe was little more than a wooden sawhorse. Its elongation, without an open plain and the highest branch of a giraffe thorn to crop, struck me as mildly grotesque.

More than mere organism, an animal gets constituted in its essential activities of perceiving and doing. The biologist Jakob von Uexküll describes the organized experience of a particular creature as its *Umwelt*, a German compound meaning "a surrounding world" or "milieu." In his essay "A Stroll through the Worlds of Animals and Men," he explains,

> We are easily deluded into assuming that the relationship between a foreign subject and the objects in his world exists on the same spatial and temporal plane as our own relations with the objects in our human world. This fallacy is fed by a belief in the existence of a single world, into which all living creatures are pigeonholed. This gives rise to the widespread conviction that there is only one space and one time for all living things. Only recently have physicists begun to doubt the existence of a universe with a space that is valid for all beings.

The *Umwelt* of which von Uexküll writes is not a shared environment but an entirely subjective, phenomenal world. We can enter the *Umwelt* of another creature — its particular world of time and space, cause and effect — only through imaginative forays. Though taken up through analogy as a military term, *foray* finds its roots in foraging. Just so, a squirrel leaves the tree trunk to seek out a crust of bread on our deck, ventures onto a sill, and finds itself staring through our kitchen window.

———

In the year after my parents divorced, when I was nine and my sister ten, my mother brought two baby squirrels home from work. Their drey of leaves and dog hair had been dislodged by a downpour, leaving the babies in a gutter. Their skin was still pink and hairless, loose on their tiny skeletons and soft as silk. With neither sight nor hearing yet, they moved but slightly and trembled a great deal. We fed them formula with an eyedropper and kept them in a shoebox lined with washcloths. Only one survived, which we named Sequoya, after the famous Cherokee leader.

After seven weeks, we moved Sequoya into a cage on

our back porch. We began to introduce husked sunflower seeds and acorns into her diet. June afternoons, my sister and I would set her at the base of an oak: she instinctively clutched the bark and soon learned to move a few feet up and down. Mr. Dickerson, who tended a small farm across the street, leaned on his hoe to watch us. He could cure a sick hen or dowse for water, but he simply shrugged when we asked him how to raise a squirrel. "They make good eating," he said wistfully.

By September, when school resumed, we could leave the cage open, letting her wander the trees all day. At dusk we would whistle her in. By November, she no longer came back at night but still returned for the mast we left out each morning. Even years later, however wild, she would approach gingerly to snatch walnuts from our palms.

In the coming years, we would move to a house at the center of town, leaving Sequoya behind. But aware of our success, people brought us more squirrels found after storms. I would occasionally carry one to school in the large pocket of my parka, a hidden presence through the dull round of algebra or civics.

In the tenth grade, after having my wisdom teeth removed, I was allowed to stay home for several days, stretched on the couch with a juvenile squirrel on my chest. On the television, Foghorn Leghorn chased Henery Hawk around the corner of a farmhouse to the tune of "Camptown Races." Floating on a pleasant cloud of codeine, my reflexes and respiration were calm and slow, my brain at the frost point of thought. By contrast, the squirrel clutched my shirt with protracted claws, its whole frame tense, its heart fluttering. Slow and fast, we sat that way through the afternoon, our lives lived on different frequencies.

Our final litter of squirrels ended badly. Listless and congested, they could hardly swallow formula and let it trickle out the sides of their mouths. Their slack bellies shrank, and it proved difficult to keep them warm. My mother brought a bottle of chloroform home from the pharmacy. We poured some onto a napkin and held it against the first squirrel's muzzle. When its body went slack, I held it in a bucket of water until the squirrel was drowned. After anesthetizing the second squirrel, I likewise held it underwater. But it suddenly came to life with frenzied energy, twisting against my hand. With such a will to survive, it might well have outlived its sickly infancy. But having gone so far, with some horror, I snapped its neck.

Such childhood experiences with animals must be both traumatic and commonplace. Our first experience of responsibility often involves delicate and short-lived pets: parakeets collide with mirrors, hamsters escape to starve in heating vents, cats get hit by dump trucks. Still earlier, with stuffed animals and animated cartoons, we rehearse such relationships, testing the possibilities of friendship and responsibility. Our imagination for suffering begins with small creatures, envoys of life and extinction.

There are subjective facts, worlds of feeling, of which we on the outside can have little ken. When a dream or memory directs our waking life—when a chicken sees the shadow of a hawk where it once struck and so avoids that corner of the yard—no amount of observation from the outside would be likely to reveal its root cause. Von Uexküll argues that the reality of each creature is, in this sense, intensely subjective:

There are, then, purely subjective realities in the *Umwelten*; and even the things that exist objectively in the environment never appear there as their objective selves. They are always transformed into perceptual cues or perceptual images and invested with a functional tone. This alone makes them into real objects, although no element of the functional tone is actually present in the stimuli.

Conversely, cause and effect often lie beyond the horizon of the subjective world, the flash of an automobile in a squirrel's eye. Though founded through ignorance or error, such limits are real and determining. As the poet John Tipton writes in "Chinati," "here bald red-headed buzzards eat / a rabbit struck by what / it only understood as supernatural." The divide between subjective reality and objective fact—between rabbit consciousness and offending vehicle—or between one subjective reality and another, finds no resolution in the natural sciences. It can properly be called magic.

In Shaw Nature Reserve, southwest of St. Louis, I step across the threshold of the forest and sit on a large rock to eat a sandwich. My eyes slowly adjust to the dim light, my ears to the quiet. A gray squirrel rustles around the base of a red oak some ten yards away. It tucks an acorn in its mouth, then freezes for a moment, alert to my presence. Hopping forward, it digs furtively with its front paws, shoves its muzzle in the hole, and quickly covers it over. But the effort is a feint, a game of cups. The squirrel moves a few yards away, digs another hole, and thrusts the acorn in with its whole body.

The forest floor must be pocked with feints and scattered caches as numerous as craters in the moon. It has long been assumed that squirrels forget their locations, blithely dispersing acorns without advantage. Yet recent research suggests that the squirrel's brain—itself the size of an acorn—holds a map of these caches by which it plots a course through the winter months. The possibility, like the ghostly chalking of a geometric equation, exceeds my comprehension. Meanwhile, the squirrel in question recedes into a thicket. I stand up, brush the crumbs from my pants, and head for the car.

Sycamores and Sleep

Having spent the morning shut up inside, I step outdoors, into the thin afternoon light of winter. Henry David Thoreau regularly equated houses with tombs, "the architecture of the grave." My street proves quiet and peaceful as a cemetery today as I walk between rows of houses, breathing in cold air, shaking my mind free of dust.

From the eastern edge of Tower Grove Park, I gaze down a long, rolling field lined with trees. Sycamores stand out among the walnuts, oaks, and dense alders, luminous as ivory. Some are brittle and blasted at the top, some with horizontal boughs stretching out like branch lightning. All have dirty trunks and clean white limbs. A few starlings cling to their tops like marcescent leaves, catching the afternoon sun. Squirrel dreys clog the crooks of branches.

I stop beneath one old sycamore, leaning back to follow its lines from root to tiptop. Looking up through the lattice at high cumulus clouds—moving mountain ranges—I feel a touch of vertigo. Soon these empty spaces will be filled with pale green leaves, huge and papery. In spring, the sycamore's canopy becomes grand and billowing, like the sails on a fully rigged ship. On a warm and breezy day, it can elicit the gentle euphoria of ragtime.

In *Remarks on Forest Scenery*, William Gilpin gives plane trees—referring to both American sycamores and Oriental planes of the same genus—pride of place in his epic catalogs of historic trees. He includes "the plane-tree hanging over the temple of Delphos, which Theophrastus supposes was as ancient as the times of Agamemnon"; another which Menelaus planted in Arcadia while raising forces for the Trojan War, and which Pausanias saw as late as 170 A.D.; a third by which Socrates swore oaths. In Phrygia, setting out on his invasion of mainland Greece, Xerxes became so enamored of a wonderful plane tree that he halted for three days. "His pavilion was spread under it; and he enjoyed the luxury of its delicious shade; while the Greeks were taking measures to seize the pass at Thermopylae."

The sycamore that I stand before has no such historic

pedigree, but it does have impressive girth. A smooth bole flows around one aperture, a hollow at eye level. I can just make out within the cavity, nearly three feet in diameter, a cluttered nest of leaves, pine needles, and threads of purple yarn unraveled from a scarf. How many such holes have been used as secret mail drops or hasty caches for stolen treasure? Tree hollows have a deep appeal to our imagination as both hiding spaces and primitive shelters. According to Cherokee myth, the world was cold until lightning lit a fire in the bottom of a hollow sycamore. Like Prometheus, this lightning flash brought flame from the upper world, and the middle world has had fire ever since. Yet the hollow sycamore precedes human habitation; it is a primal hearth in the midst of wilderness.

Massive brick homes line the avenues around Tower Grove Park. We who live here can feel dwarfed by our own structures, misplaced among these monuments to arid passions. In *Walden*, Thoreau warns us, "Better not keep a house. Say, some hollow tree; and then for morning calls and dinner-parties!" In his journal from 1840, he declares whimsically, "My neighbor inhabits a hollow sycamore, and I a beech tree." Thoreau kept alive the childhood dream of living in trees, finding a lair or nest in nature that would allow him to live without alienation or excess.

Nor was he alone in this fantasy. Gilpin describes a plane tree that stood in Lycia during the reign of Caesars: "From a vast stem it divided into several huge boughs ... Its branches still flourished, while its trunk decayed. This in process of time mouldered into an immense cave, at least eighty feet in circumference; around the sides of which were placed seats of pumice stone; cushioned softly with moss." The governor Licinius Mutianus feasted with eighteen of his men in this hollow. According to Pliny the Elder, the Emperor Caligula at his villa near Velitrae had an Oriental plane so large that he held a banquet in its shade, with the horizontal branches serving as additional seats. He called this dining room his "eerie" or "nest." A. J. Downing, in his *Treatise on the Theory and Practice of Landscape Gardening*, writes of a specimen of American sycamore "cut on the banks of the Genesee river, of such enormous size, that a section of the trunk was hollowed out and furnished as a small room, capable of containing fourteen persons." In "The Hollow Tree," John Clare recalls a pollard "wasted to a shell / Whose vigorous head still grew and flourished well / Where ten might sit upon the battered floor / And still look round discovering room for more." In such accounts, the trunk expands to a primitive feast hall while at the same time offering a snug retreat or nest. It is at once inside and outside, intimate and immense.

My two-year-old daughter frequently opens the children's book *I Am a Bunny* to its last page, where Nicholas sleeps through the winter in his hollow tree. In Richard Scarry's illustration, the rabbit lies on a pallet of soft straw, tucked beneath a blue blanket; his yellow shirt and red overalls hang on the tree wall. Outside, snow falls steadily through a gray sky, weighing down the branches of a fir in the distance. It's an image of living alone without loneliness, finding a warm home in the heart of the wide outdoors.

———

The park grows cold, empty of people, but a listless feeling leaves me rooted and reluctant to turn home. All is quiet but for the pop of a cracked seed, the thin song of a single cardinal, and distant cars. I peel a strip of bark from the sycamore's trunk, revealing smooth, creamy wood beneath. Year-round, the tree exfoliates, shedding itself onto the lawn. Lower down, the trunk remains partly encased in bark, whereas the upper reaches are only lightly speckled with chips or else altogether nude. Marianne Moore calls attention to this aspect of the tree in her poem "The Sycamore":

> Against a gun-metal sky
> I saw an albino giraffe. Without
> leaves to modify,
> chamois-white as
> said, although partly pied near the base,
> it towered where a chain of
> stepping-stones lay in a stream nearby;
> glamor to stir the envy
>
> of anything in motley—

Like Gerard Manley Hopkins—"Glory be to God for dappled things"—Moore is an advocate of all things brindled, freckled, mottled, and piebald. She admires the naked sycamore, yet she suggests that its unmodified brilliance proves a little imposing. Nearby, she finds a shriveled flower in the grass, "retiringly formal," bearing witness to the tree like "a field-mouse at Versailles" (as her composite poem quotes from somewhere). Next to the sycamore, it is a figure of subtlety and modesty.

Close at hand, the "partly pied" base of a sycamore is actually quite variegated, with patches of green, gray, and brown where the bark still clings. It draws the hand like few other trees, instilling an itch to chip away at the light, stiff casing. Beneath, the green wood feels waxy in finish and fibrous in texture, as if finely scored with a chisel. My fingertips find it dense and moist compared to the bark, cool to the touch, though not so cold as the air around it.

But what does the hand really know? The skin's exposed nerve endings register pressure; the distribution and intensity of pressure communicate texture (experienced as traction when the hand moves). Working in harmony, the nerve endings form an idea of smoothness through uniformity, roughness through minute variations in pressure from point to point. These nerves also feel degrees of heat and cold, where external temperature varies from that of the blood. Of the senses, touch offers the most restrictive field of information. Yet it proves imminently useful in negotiating the world. It is primal, preceding human images, our earliest sense in terms of ontogeny and phylogeny. Touch is felt by a fetus curled in the womb, just as it was felt by a primitive ancestor of the sea anemone some 630 million years ago. It occurs before the first crack of light, before the first heartbeat of sound.

As pliant armor, skin marks the limits of a self, where inside stops and outside begins. Yet it exposes the nervous system across our outer surfaces, risking contact to absorb external facts. Skin weathers wind, sun, stretching, and rubbing, constantly renewing itself to remain supple. Like a snake, the human body molts dead layers, but in sifting flakes and dust throughout the year rather than in a single sheath. Each of us sheds more than a million skin cells in a single hour. In this respect, I imagine myself—absurdly—as a soft and mobile sycamore. With my palm against a bare patch of trunk, our exposed surfaces make contact.

Though a tree has no nervous system, and presumably feels nothing, we cannot but draw analogies between bark and skin, wood and flesh. A tree organizes my experience of space, an upright figure on the horizon and a psychic center. It focuses the field of my attention as a human would, providing a sense of scale. In landscapes without trees I am as lost as I would be among ocean swells, with no familiar measure for theatrical distances.

I think of all the people in Ovid's *Metamorphoses* who change into trees, suggesting our imaginative proximity to arboreal life: the blood of Pyramus and Thisbe runs through the mulberry tree, Daphne turns to laurel, Baucis and Philemon to oak and linden, Dryope to poplar, Cyparissus to cypress, Thracian maenads to oak, and Myrrha to myrrh. Sometimes a metamorphosis offers reward for a life well lived, sometimes escape from a life gone wrong, but it always results in a life's lasting emblem. We speak of trees as alive; but compared to the frenzied rush of human existence, vegetable gradations of life seem attenuated and cool, deeply rooted in moist alluvial soil. Neither quick nor dead, in human terms, they provide a refuge resembling sleep. As Myrrha prays,

> O Goddes, if of repentant folk you any mercye take,
> Sharpe vengeance I confesse I have deserved,
>   and content
> I am to take it paciently. How bee it to the'entent

That neyther with my lyfe the quick, nor with my
  death the dead
Anoyed bee, from both of them exempt mee this
  same sted,
And altring mee, deny to mee both lyfe and death.

And so the earth closed over her feet, roots thrust from
her toes, her blood turned to watery sap, branches
stretched out from her arms, and her skin hardened into
bark. In Ovid, our fell or foolish deeds cast vast shadows
into trees, which cast in turn their shadows back on us.

On a damp morning in early March, I approach the
same sycamore while strolling through the park. The
tree shines, pale as a marble column in the thinning fog.
At its base, a raccoon stoops over a braid of roots, caught
out in daylight and looking stunned. It must be old or
sick or injured, to stand so exposed. The creature col-
lects its last energy for the five-foot climb to the hole. Its
hunched posture and unfocused eyes suggest an animal
mind in revolt against the facts to which it was born.

When I pass again, the raccoon has stolen away—up,

I hope, into the hollow tree. When Odysseus washes ashore in Phaeacia, to sleep exhausted in a bed of leaves, Homer describes him as a hidden ember:

> In the midst he lay,
> Store of leaves heaping high on every side.
> And as in some out-field a man doth hide
> A kindld brand to keepe the seed of fire,
> No neighbour dwelling neare, and his desire
> Serv'd with selfe store he else would aske of none,
> But of his fore-spent sparks rakes th' ashes on:
> So this out-place Ulysses thus receives;
> And thus nak't vertue's seed lies hid in leaves.

I imagine the raccoon curled in just such a rough nest within the sycamore, deep in animal slumber, itself its own hearth and Promethean fire.

Mouse God

The first warm day of spring, we open the windows wide, hang carpets across the fence, and clean house. A high ceiling of cumulus cloud drifts slowly eastward, scrolling the sky. A neighbor lathers and rinses her malamute beneath a garden hose, while down the street, the thin whine of a circular saw makes a fuss about improving things.

In this century-old brick house, our rooms have been dark through the winter. Terrarium light filters through a massive holly tree outside the living-room window. Streaky panes look out on the tree's interior, where a mockingbird sits close to the trunk during snowfall, guarding its berries. In the scene's preternatural silence and weird illumination, it resembles a diorama in some natural history museum. But today, the mockingbird perches atop a stop sign at the end of the block, its tail cocked, menacing all comers. In our front hall, a light breeze flips pages of a magazine.

I work with zeal, taking mental inventory of each room, returning luster to wood surfaces, reacquainting myself with vast stretches of yellow-pine floorboards, vacuuming up the pale, airy dust from corners, day-dreaming all the while. I begin on the ground floor of common sense but soon ascend into abstraction or descend into the dim cellar of childhood memories, a little dehydrated by the end of it. Household dust is largely composed, I have heard, of human skin and hair, in addition to dog fur, particles of plaster, fibers from rugs, and dirt blown in from the street. Our exfoliated remains lose color; the past turns the present ghostly gray. To account for the composition of dust, and to clean well, one must work with a magnifying glass, on hands and knees. Usually, only children get so close to things.

Henry David Thoreau expressed disdain for our servitude to the structures we inhabit, which come to resemble workhouses, labyrinths, museums, prisons, and mausoleums. Of furniture, he writes in *Walden*,

> At present our houses are cluttered and defiled with it, and a good housewife would sweep out the greater part into the dust hole, and not leave her morning's work undone. Morning work! By the blushes of Aurora and

the music of Memnon, what should be man's *morning work* in this world? I had three pieces of limestone on my desk, but I was terrified to find that they required to be dusted daily, when the furniture of my mind was all undusted still, and I threw them out the window in disgust. How, then, could I have a furnished house? I would rather sit in the open air, for no dust gathers on the grass, unless where man has broken ground.

I could not refute Thoreau's sense of economy, nor would I resist his advocacy of open air. Out walking, I have sometimes passed a gaudy *faux château* and thought, I would rather sleep under a rhododendron. Yet I have rarely shared his feeling in regard to dusting, a masculine distaste for "morning work." Cleaning acts to placate household gods, extirpating ghosts, bringing with it the pleasures of penance.

After Odysseus has slaughtered the suitors on Apollo's feast day, he bids his unfaithful servants "clense each boord and Throne / With wetted Sponges." Then, proceeding with horrifying efficiency, he hangs the servants themselves and fumigates the hall with "All-ill-expelling Brimstone and some fire, / That, with perfumes cast, he might make entire / The house's first integrity in all." As

Jane Harrison explains, "His method of purifying is a simple and natural one, it might be adopted today in the disinfecting of a polluted house." It combines the practical demands of hygiene with the psychic need to make a fresh start.

———

Dusting, I experience the soft resonance of familiar things. Surfaces assume a lambent glow, reflecting the blur of my face. Room by room, I restore not just order but my relationship to the house. Intimate and reciprocal, I am in it, and it is in me.

My progress slows when I reach our battered piano, pressing down atonal chord clusters as I clean the keys. On its top sits a cut-glass candelabrum, now electrified, possibly French in origin, inspired by a Christmas tree or horn of plenty. It is radiant with teardrops, purple-tinted clusters of grapes, and wine-tinted apples, all of which make a soft chink beneath my dusting rag. This oddity was passed down to me from my great-grandmother, Agnes, no lamb of god but a tyrannical matriarch who persisted through iron will into her hundreds. With its lost pair, it may have sat atop a sideboard in her townhouse in Atlanta or, further back, on her father's estate in Hazelhurst, Mississippi, itself once a slave plantation. The past recedes to a distant point, a reflection in a dimple of glass.

Most objects in the house have a more ordinary provenance: a kitchen table abandoned by friends departing for the West Coast; a couch purchased at the Goodwill on Milwaukee Avenue in Chicago, still exhaling the faint odor of Lysol; an end table found in an alley, with water rings interlocked across its top (the symbol of Olympic drinking). Yet every stick of furniture must carry its own "Legend of the True Cross" stretching back through carpentry shops and lumber mills to a stand of living trees. As I run my dust cloth over a molded baseboard, I picture in my mind's eye a walnut tree deep in the Ozarks, a woodpecker's tap resounding through its solid trunk. Matter accrues secret histories to which we are only partly privy. Our props outlast us, stubbornly persisting into new lives.

In the process of cleaning, I stumble on evidence of tiny intruders. From one corner of the dining room, I collect insect larvae hidden like opals in their cottony pouches. From another, I sweep up mouse droppings, tiny black grains scattered around a gnawed chip of packing material. Through thin cracks, forces from outside creep in with the cold.

Four years ago, at the bottom of the cellar stairs, we found a pair of tiny mice, glutted with grass seed from an open bag of Kentucky bluegrass blend. After dancing around unsteadily, they proved so full and docile that we easily scooped them up in a trashcan. At the bottom, each mouse huddled in its soft fur, grayish brown on the back and buff on the belly. When I carried them upstairs, sunlight revealed a fine down on their tails. Their eyes were large and watchful, like those of field mice in children's picture books. Checking a mammal guide, we identified our visitors not as house mice but as deer mice. Whereas house mice invaded the New World on ships of Spanish conquistadors, deer mice are native to this region, thriving in Missouri's mix of woodland and prairie. Eventually, we released our pair in Tower Grove Park. In a flash, they dodged through a cluster of tulips and out of sight.

Each winter, deer mice have come back—whether

the same or others, I have no means to judge. They nose under the door or squeeze through quarter-inch cracks in our cellar walls, less welcome with each return. Poor climbers, they travel along the level top of our stone foundation. From tarry splinters of subflooring, woven with skeins of lint, they have constructed a nest just beneath the joists. The exterior of this small mass bristles, but the interior may well be lined with shredded cloth or dog fur. Countless broods may have crawled from it, though Pliny the Elder believed that mice generate spontaneously from the earth, their hoards congealing in muddy riverbeds. From this lair, led by a keen sense of smell, the mice climb ten inches to a gap between boards, offering egress to the kitchen pantry.

Last December, poking around for a snack, I found a packet of Ritz crackers gnawed open, crumbs scattered across the pantry floor. Even through cardboard and wax paper, the mice were drawn to this rich cache of salt crystals and carbohydrates. I carefully sealed our food in plastic tubs on high shelves, an embargo in our cold war. But the following night, a mouse chewed through a recipe written on index cards and kept on a low shelf with our cookbooks. Either its pleasure in food had become vicarious or else it detected savory splatters of cooking oil on the cards. Elsewhere, I discovered toothmarks across an electrical cord and a small half-moon eaten out of a record sleeve.

We rarely heard or saw these stealthy intruders. Yet every dark corner now came alive to our imaginations. Retiring to bed, we surrendered the ground floor of common sense to hidden forces. One night in the dead of winter, pricked awake by an anxious dream, I shuffled downstairs to the kitchen for a glass of water. Flicking on the light, I found a deer mouse frozen in panic on the floor, forefoot suspended midstride. The sudden manifestation of this creature—tiny yet intense—carried an uncanny charge. _Unheimlich,_ the German for "uncanny," literally means "unhomely," something from outside that has crept indoors. Ears tipped forward, whiskers trembling, the mouse seemed to gauge the expanse of linoleum between us. A second later, it vanished beneath the stove.

In "To a Mouse," the Scottish poet Robert Burns describes a similar encounter, albeit one of warmer fellow feeling. After he has turned up a nest with his plow one November, his poem takes the form of an apology:

Wee, sleeket, cowran, tim'rous *beastie*,
O, what a panic's in thy breastie!
Thou need na start awa sae hasty,
   Wi' bickering brattle!
I wad be laith to rin an' chase thee,
   Wi' murd'ring *pattle*!

I'm truly sorry Man's dominion
Has broken Nature's social union,
An' justifies that ill opinion,
   Which makes thee startle,
At me, thy poor, earth-born companion,
   An' *fellow-mortal*!

The farmer feels like an intruder in his own field, such is his sympathetic concern for the "tim'rous beastie" whose home he has destroyed. Affectionately, Rabbie Burns rhymes "breastie" with "beastie," Scots endearments and diminutives. Dust to dust, the farmer and harvest mouse are "earth-born" companions. They experience the same misfortunes in life, despite the nested hierarchies of Linnaeus. All that separates them is a conception of time. While the mouse dwells in present troubles, "I *backward* cast my e'e, / On prospects drear! / An' *forward*, tho' I canna *see*, / I *guess* an' *fear*!"

For many ancient cultures, mice offered a metonym for ruin. Their very size suggested that the sources and symptoms of disaster can be subtle. Both Leviticus and the Egyptian Book of the Dead revile mice as an abomination, apprehending a connection between rodents and bubonic plague long before bacteriology. The ancient Greeks recognized this connection as well. Following a homeopathic logic, they ascribed to mice apotropaic powers against the very plague they carried.

In Bronze Age Troas—northwestern Anatolia, the region of Troy—a cult of Apollo worshipped mice as sacred. According to legend, Teucer emigrated from Crete to settle the region. He was told by an oracle to stop wherever the "earth-born" attacked him. Sleeping one night in the open, his company was swarmed by field mice, which chewed through bowstrings and the leather handles of shields. Obeying the oracle, Teucer founded a town on the spot and named it Sminthium, the Cretan word for a mouse being *sminthos* (as the geographer Strabo informs us). He built a temple to

Apollo Smintheus, mouse god. White mice lived in holes beneath its altar, fed by priests in a solemn rite.

Apollo Smintheus remains familiar to us through the *Iliad.* At the epic's opening, Agamemnon enslaves the beautiful daughter of Chryses, priest of the mouse god, and refuses any ransom. Chryses prays,

> O Smintheus, if crownd
> With thankfull offerings thy rich Phane I ever saw,
>   or fir'd
> Fat thighs of oxen and of goates to thee, this grace
>   desir'd
> Vouchsafe to me: paines for my teares let these rude
>   Greekes repay,
> Forc'd with thy arrowes.

Smintheus answers this prayer after the manner of rodents, spreading through the Greek army a plague transmitted on the tips of his arrows. In Chryses's temple, nearly a thousand years after the fall of Troy, Scopas carved Apollo with a mouse beneath his foot. Coins from the region depict the god cupping the little creature in his hand. So intimate were god and mouse, prophecy and plague.

One morning, a newspaper article on the Sin Nombre virus catches my eye. Symptoms include rapid heart rate, hyperventilation, and cardiovascular shock. Rare but potentially deadly, the illness spreads through the droppings of deer mice. Doubtless, our house contains particulate matter of their fur and feces mixed with human sheddings. Night and day, we must inhale this fine dust.

Leaving for a visit to the Scottish Borders, I set across the kitchen floor half a dozen mousetraps baited with peanut butter. By the time we return, four of them have snapped, flipped by force upside down. Each sprung bar has crushed a neck or spine, eyes bulging from its pressure. I lift the traps gingerly by the edges and drop them in a Dumpster. Undertaking done, I wash my hands, mop the floor, and open a bottle of beer. After a month of cold, our house ticks with the furnace's soft explosion. Late-afternoon sunlight shines on wet linoleum. The smell of pine cleanser makes entire "the house's first integrity in all."

Owl Light

Clear Cymric voices carry well this autumn night,
Aneurin and Taliesin, cruel owls
for whom it is never altogether dark, crying
before the rules made poetry a pedant's game.

BASIL BUNTING, "Briggflatts"

Some days never fully darken, arrested at twilight. Low cloud cover reflects the orange glow of sodium lamps, as if lit by a pale fire. The buildings on our block cast thin shadows, darkness pooling under lintels and eaves. On such a night, as I stand with my back to the house, a great horned owl glides overhead, silent on soft-edged feathers. Wings outstretched, it settles for a moment on a dead branch. The bird nods its tufted head a few times, triangulating distance, or else catching the frequencies of some furtive scratching. With a single stroke, it launches downward, swooping within a few feet of the ground. I lose sight of it behind a neighbor's garage, but I imagine the huge talons grasping flesh or air.

The coming of night coincides for owls with hunger, working on them as an agitation. Asleep on their roosts through the morning hours, they begin to stir as shadows lengthen toward dusk. One winter afternoon, we spot a barred owl hunched in an oak, at the western edge of city sprawl. It glances our way, eyes entirely black, filled with a fluid leeched from darkness. Hooting, "who cooks for you," its head bobs up and down with each note, feathers rippling like fur or water, restless for night to fall. As we rise to leave, the owl turns toward us one more time, peering through the bare knothole of its face.

Like primates, but few other creatures, owls have clearly demarcated faces, with forward-facing eyes set in a flat disc. There, one finds the rudiments of human features, but without recognizable expression. As in wooden masks of the Kwakiutl, owl eyes glint from behind a rigid surface, encased in feathers. Camouflaged, the owl often disappears against the bole of a tree, leaving only eyes visible. William Blake told George Richmond, "I can look at a knot in a piece of wood till I am frightened at it." Perhaps he was seeing an owl.

For three weeks, I have been observing a pair of great horned owls in Tower Grove Park. This morning, perched in a thick stand of pines, they resemble huge seedpods or beehives, motionless but alert. Crouching directly beneath, I can make out the fine ribs of feathers splayed across each breast, tawny stripes across an undertone of milk white. I step away from the trees and find the larger of the two, the female, staring at me through a gap between branches. From her upright tufts, feathered brows—like the brows of a Northumbrian bard—angle downward across her face to form a severe V. In order to get a better look, I shift ten paces to the right and raise my binoculars: the owl's unblinking eyes remain fixed on me, chrome yellow around the pupils. I am more watched than watcher.

Returning a little after noon, I find the same owl snoozing on her roost. She looks almost jolly while asleep, eyes shut tight against the sun, slate-black bill tucked trimly into her feathered face. Sleeping rigidly upright, the bird seems not so much loosened from care as concentrated in satisfaction.

From the roost, some small weight crashes lightly through pine needles. Kicking around in the shadows, I discover an owl pellet, leaden in color, cast off after last night's feast. Its mush includes clumps of fur, feather barbs, the upper mandible of a songbird, and shards of a tiny femur. Digging deeper in the dry needles, I turn up hundreds of bone fragments, the accumulation of years or even decades. This ossuary forms a record of indigestible facts, a noctuary of ravening. In scope and repetition, these notched bones entail an owl epic, like the wrecked banquets and broken lances of which Aneurin (or Aneirin) sang, numbering the dead:

> A man went to Catraeth at dawn,
> Lordly face like a shield-wall.
> Sharply they'd attack, they'd gather spoils,
> Loud as thunder the crash of shields.
> Ardent man, prudent man, singular man,
> He'd rip and he'd pierce with spear-points.
> Deep in blood he would strike with blades,
> Hard-pressed, steel weapons on heads.

Owls get occluded by poetry and myth, lost in twilit language. The living bird gives way to a portent of death and evil, a symbol of occult knowledge. Its "lugubrious cries" and "sad complaints" need no rehearsal, so familiar are their sinister associations from literature. As Puck declares in A *Midsummer Night's Dream*, by way of saying good night, "Now the wasted brands do glow, / Whilst the screech-owl, screeching loud, / Puts the wretch that lies in woe / In remembrance of a shroud."

In ancient Greece, the owl perched on Athena's shoulder as a symbol of wisdom and war. Some have argued that Athena was herself a personification of twilight, when owls begin their hunt. In the murky recesses of Greek religion, the goddess crossed paths with the Gorgon Medusa and thereafter bore the severed head on her aegis. Medusa may in fact have been a terrifying aspect of Athena that the Homeric age decapitated from all but a few cults. Gorgoneia, masklike images of the Gorgon's head, continued to hang on the ovens of bakers and potters, often beside images of Athena's bird. Gorgoneia have huge googly eyes, much like those of an owl. Anyone who has met the fierce gaze of an owl might well believe it could—like the Gorgon—turn flesh to stone.

Sophocles twice refers to Athena as "Gorgon-eyed," but her more common epithet is *glaukōpis*, meaning "bright-eyed" or "with flashing eyes." The word is a compound of *glaukos*, "gleaming" or "gray," and *ōps*, "eye" or "face." *Glaux*, "owl," derives from the same root as *glaukos*, and some scholars have translated *glaukōpis* as "owl-eyed." Excavating Hissarlik, or Troy, in the late nineteenth century, Heinrich Schliemann unearthed idols of Athena from the lower strata. These figurines had human limbs but round owl faces with menacing brows. In Homer's epics, Athena takes human form, only figuratively owlish, yet she seems to have been theriomorphic in ancient Troy. Back and further back, in the prehistoric dark, perhaps this goddess was an owl, every owl an instance of divinity.

Beyond signs and wonders, what hold do their beaks and talons have on our consciousness? In a brief poem from the 1930s, Lorine Niedecker attempts to dispense with poetic and mythic associations in order to give us a real owl:

A monster owl
out on the fence
flew away. What
is it the sign
of? The sign of
an owl.

The word "monster" raises the specter of Gothic fantasy, but Niedecker quickly undercuts any portentous possibilities. With common sense and brusque humor, she declares that the owl is only a sign of itself, an identity in the mathematical sense of the word. Yet we are still in the realm of signification rather than being, talking indoors rather than "out on the fence." The owl itself eludes us.

———

At 5 p.m., I find the great horned owls perched at the edge of a field, vigorously preening. They slide their beaks through a fringe of wing feathers, extended necks surprisingly supple. The male leans forward to clean his talons, lifting one leg at a time to meet his beak. With eyes shut tight, he gingerly combs a claw against his feline head, a gesture familiar from house cats. In Mandarin Chinese, an owl is called *mao tou ying*, literally, "cat-headed hawk." The name perfectly captures the chimerical nature of this creature, a hybrid of otherwise incongruous aspects.

Dark begins to fall. Beside a picnic shelter, a drunk man vomits violently, doubled over in his camouflage jacket. The owls seem to pay him no heed; but suddenly, the female opens her wings and enters a long swoop, the field pouring away in her wake. Her flight is graceful and efficient, yet a large event, like a schooner under sail. With talons extended, she lands in a sycamore, intently focused on the field beyond. A distant mockingbird, singing too late, may dilate in her eye, its throat pulsing with song. The two owls exchange rounded vowels, low tones of a friction drum. The male follows to the sycamore, from which they both take flight. As Basil Bunting observes, for owls, "it is never altogether dark." But I can see no more than two darker patches of the general darkness, saturated black against the grass. They soon merge with woods beyond, where no human sense can follow.

The next morning, I cut across the park, traveling in a socket of luminous fog. No trucks rumble past; no birds sing. At the edge of a blurry field, in the mud, I find what's left of an exploded mockingbird. A halo of feathers surrounds the ravaged remains—brain gone, astonished eye still in its head.

Works Cited

Adamson, Robert. "Crows in Afternoon Sunlight." In *Mulberry Leaves: New and Selected Poems, 1970–2001*, edited by Chris Edwards. Sydney: Paper Bark Press, 2001.

Aneirin. *The Gododdin*. Translated by Joseph P. Clancy. In *The Triumph Tree: Scotland's Earliest Poetry, 550–1350*, edited by Thomas Owen Clancy. Edinburgh: Canongate Books, 1998.

Arnold, Matthew. *Culture and Anarchy*. Edited by Samuel Lipman. New Haven, Conn.: Yale University Press, 1994.

Blake, William. *The Marriage of Heaven and Hell*. New York: Dover, 1994.

Blake Records. Edited by G. E. Bentley, Jr. Oxford: Oxford University Press, 1969.

Bunting, Basil. "Briggflatts." In *Complete Poems*, edited by Richard Caddel. New York: New Directions, 2003.

Burke, Kenneth. "Literature as Equipment for Living." In *The Philosophy of Literary Form*. 3rd ed. Berkeley: University of California Press, 1973.

Burns, Robert. "To a Mouse, on Turning Her Up in Her Nest, with the Plough, November, 1785." In *Burns: Poems and*

Songs, edited by James Kinsley. London: Oxford University Press, 1969.

Burroughs, John. *Squirrels and Other Fur-Bearers*. Boston: Houghton Mifflin, 1900.

Catullus. Carmen III. In *C. Valerii Catulli Carmina*, edited by R. A. B. Mynors. Oxford: Clarendon Press, 1958.

Clare, John. "The Hollow Tree." In *Selected Poems and Prose of John Clare*, edited by Eric Robinson and Geoffrey Summerfield. Oxford: Oxford University Press, 1978.

Downing, A. J. *A Treatise on the Theory and Practice of Landscape Gardening, Adapted to North America; with a View to the Improvement of Country Residences ... with Remarks on Rural Architecture*. 6th ed. New York: A. O. Moore and Company, 1859.

Duncan, Robert. "Roots and Branches." In *Roots and Branches*. New York: Charles Scribner's Sons, 1964.

Gilpin, William. *Remarks on Forest Scenery, and Other Woodland Views (Relative Chiefly to Picturesque Beauty), Illustrated by the Scenes of New-Forest in Hampshire*. 2nd ed. Vol. 1. London: R. Blamire, 1794.

Harrison, Jane Ellen. *Prolegomena to the Study of Greek Religion*. Princeton, N.J.: Princeton University Press, 1991.

Herakleitos. In *Seven Greeks: Translations by Guy Davenport*. New York: New Directions, 1995.

Herrick, Robert. "To the Most Fair and Lovely Mistris Anne Soame, Now Lady Abdie." In *Hesperides and Noble Num-*

bers, edited by Ernest Rhys. London: J. M. Dent and Sons, 1923.

Higgins, Aidan. "The Other Day I Was Thinking of You." In *Flotsam and Jetsam*. Normal, Ill.: Dalkey Archive Press, 2002.

Homer. *Chapman's Homer: The Iliad, The Odyssey, and the Lesser Homerica*. 2 vols. Translated by George Chapman and edited by Allardyce Nicoll. New York: Princeton University Press, 1967.

Hopkins, Gerard Manley. "Pied Beauty." In *Poems and Prose*. New York: Penguin Books, 1985.

Kirk, Robert. *The Secret Commonwealth: Of Elves, Fauns, and Fairies*. Introduction by Marina Warner. New York: New York Review Books, 2007.

Martin, Laura C. *The Folklore of Birds*. Old Saybrook, Conn.: Globe Pequot Press, 1993.

Moore, Marianne. "The Sycamore." In *Complete Poems*. New York: Penguin Books, 1981.

Niedecker, Lorine. "A monster owl." In *Collected Works*, edited by Jenny Penberthy. Berkeley: University of California Press, 2002.

Ovid. *Metamorphoses: The Arthur Golding Translation, 1567*. Edited by John Frederick Nims. New York: Macmillan, 1965.

Pickard, Tom. "Dusk." In *Hole in the Wall: New and Selected Poems*. Chicago: Flood Editions, 2002.

Plotinus. *The Enneads*. Translated by Stephen MacKenna. New York: Penguin Books, 1991.

Poe, Edgar Allan. "The Raven." In *The Collected Tales and Poems of Edgar Allan Poe*. New York: Modern Library, 1992.

Proust, Marcel. *Swann's Way*. Translated by C. K. Scott Moncrieff. New York: Vintage Books, 1989.

Rosen, Jonathan. "Flight Patterns." *New York Times*, 22 April 2007.

Scott, Walter. *Letters on Demonology and Witchcraft*. Ware, Hertfordshire: Wordsworth Editions, 2001.

Temps critiques [Jacques Guigou and Jacques Wajnsztejn]. "Hard blocking." *Temps critiques* 14 (April 2006): 33–40.

Thomson, James. "Sunday Up the River." In *The Poetical Works of James Thomson: The City of Dreadful Night, Vane's Story, Voice from the Nile, Weddah and Om-El-Bonain, and Poetical Remains*, vol. 1, edited by Bertram Dobell. London: Reeves and Turner, 1895.

Thoreau, Henry David. *The Journal*. Vol. 1. Edited by Bradford Torrey and F. H. Allen. New York: Dover, 1962.

———. *Walden and Civil Disobedience*. New York: Penguin Books, 1983.

Tipton, John. "Chinati." In *Photos: Poems 1.2004–3.2005*. Chicago: privately printed, 2005.

Turin, Luca. "Note to: Quest Perfumers, December 14, 1996." Quoted in Chandler Burr, *The Emperor of Scent: A Story of Perfume, Obsession, and the Last Mystery of the Senses* (New York: Random House, 2002), 207.

"The Twa Corbies." In *Border Ballads: A Selection*, edited by James Reed. Manchester, U.K.: Carcanet Press, 1991.

Uexküll, Jakob von. "A Stroll through the Worlds of Animals and Men." In *Instinctive Behavior: The Development of a Modern Concept*, translated and edited by Claire H. Schiller. New York: International Universities Press, 1957.

West, Meredith J., and Andrew P. King. "Mozart's Starling." *American Scientist* 78 (March–April 1990): 106–14.

Yeats, William Butler. *The Collected Works of W. B. Yeats, Volume I: The Poems*. Rev. ed. Edited by Richard J. Finneran. New York: Macmillan, 1989.

———. *Reveries over Childhood and Youth*. In *The Collected Works of W. B. Yeats, Volume III: Autobiographies*, edited by William O'Donnell and Douglas Archibald. New York: Scribner, 1999.

Born in 1970, Devin Johnston is the author of three books of poetry: *Sources* (Turtle Point Press, 2008), *Aversions* (Omnidawn, 2004) and *Telepathy* (Paper Bark Press, 2001). His book of criticism, *Precipitations: Contemporary American Poetry as Occult Practice*, appeared from Wesleyan University Press in 2002. He co-directs Flood Editions, an independent publishing house, and teaches at Saint Louis University.